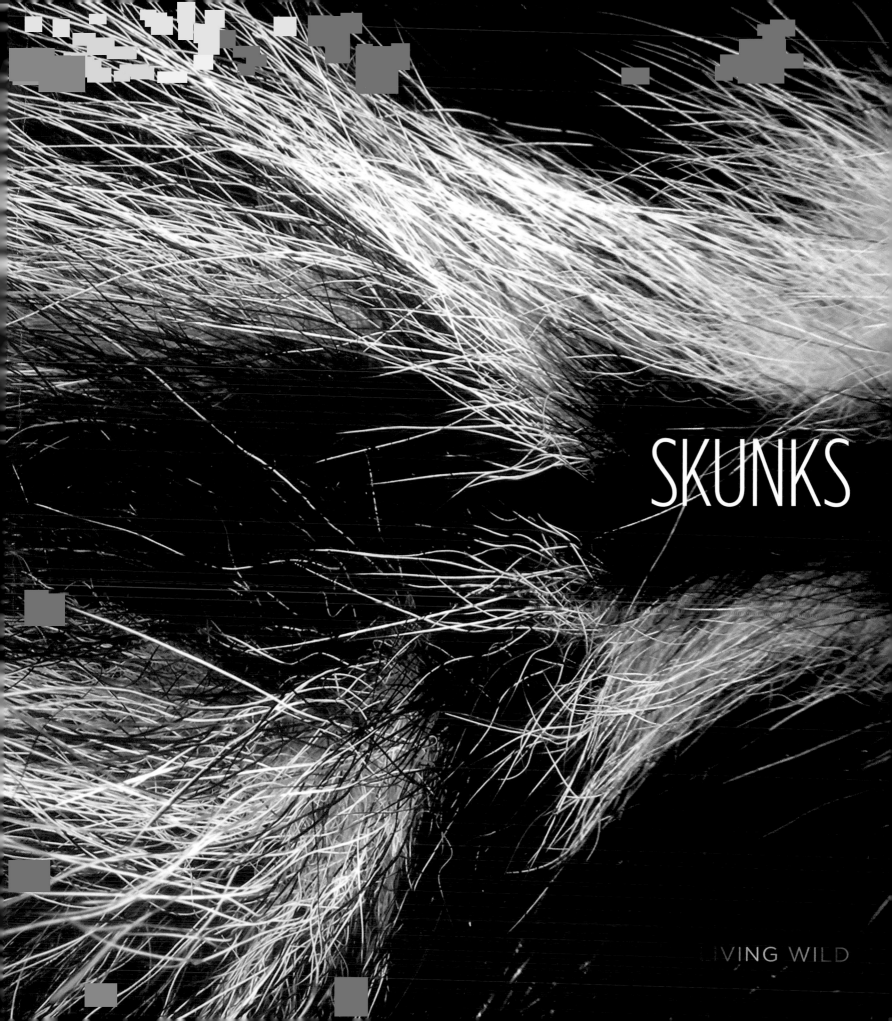

SKUNKS

LIVING WILD

Published by Creative Education
P.O. Box 227, Mankato, Minnesota 56002
Creative Education is an imprint of The Creative Company
www.thecreativecompany.us

Design and production by Mary Herrmann
Art direction by Rita Marshall
Printed in the United States of America

Photographs by 123rf (graphiquez, Jent Kyle, Shirley Palmer, pictureguy66), Alamy (AF archive, Arco Images GmbH, Victor Savushkin), Dreamstime (Sergejus Byckovskis, Outdoorsman, Michael Robbins), Getty Images (altrendo nature, Comstock Images, Daniel Cox, Tim Fitzharris, STEVE MASLOWSKI, Leonard Lee Rue III, Gerard Soury), iStockphoto (Stacy Able, Silvia Boratti), Shutterstock (Anne-Marie B, azaphoto, dotweb, Cynthia Kidwell, Heiko Kiera, Geoffrey Kuchera, Eduard Kyslynskyy, Patsy Michaud, Ryan Morgan, Pictureguy, Jamie Roach, Becky Sheridan, Berit Ullmann, Danny Xu), Wikipedia (AnimalPhotos, A. E. Brehm, Caspian, Keven Law, Hugh Manatee, NASA, NPS)

Library of Congress Cataloging-in-Publication Data
Gish, Melissa.
Skunks / by Melissa Gish.
p. cm. — (Living wild)
Includes index.
Summary: A look at skunks, including their habitats, physical characteristics such as their odorous musk, behaviors, relationships with humans, and common status in the world today.
ISBN 978-1-60818-290-9
1. Skunks—Juvenile literature. I. Title.

QL737.C248G57 2013
599.76'8—dc23   2012023246

9 8 7 6 5 4 3 2

CREATIVE EDUCATION

SKUNKS

Melissa Gish

In the early August breeze, a stand of slender
yellow birch sways in New Hampshire. As the

sun sets, five skunks—a mother and her four offspring—emerge from a burrow on a hillside.

In the early August breeze, a stand of slender yellow birch sways behind a farmstead fence in New Hampshire. As the sun sets, five skunks—a mother and her four offspring—emerge from a burrow on a hillside. Only recently have the young given up their mother's milk in favor of grasshoppers and wild strawberries. The skunks march through the grass, the mother pausing occasionally to sniff the air for any sign of danger. Under a thorny bush, she finds overripe blackberries scattered on the ground. The young skunks gather around their mother to feast on the succulent fruit. From its perch on a tree branch high above, a great gray owl watches this activity with calm interest— waiting. Following a trail of berries to a neighboring bush, one of the young skunks leaves the protection of its mother. The owl takes the opportunity and silently glides earthward, talons prepared to strike.

WHERE IN THE WORLD THEY LIVE

■ **Hooded Skunk**
American
Southwest

■ **Spotted Skunk**
United States,
Mexico

■ **Stink Badger**
Philippines,
Indonesia

■ **Striped Skunk**
throughout North
America

Hog-nosed Skunk
Colorado, New
Mexico, Texas,
Mexico

The 12 skunk species are classified as belonging to 5 different groups, and the colored squares on this page represent common locations of those groups. Skunk populations are concentrated in certain parts of the world, from the Asian stink badgers to the hooded skunks of the American Southwest. Striped and spotted skunks are more common throughout North America, while hog-nosed skunks have a more restricted range.

SPOTS OR STRIPES

Scientists once classified skunks as belonging to the weasel family, but new research has determined that skunks are a distinct family. The 12 species of skunk comprise the family called Mephitinae (*meh-FY-tih-nay*), named for a Latin word meaning "stink." Although all carnivorous **mammals** have scent glands near the anus, which the animals typically use for smearing scent markers on territory boundaries, the skunk family has the unique ability to spray its odorous **musk**. The name "skunk" originated in the Algonquian word *segonku*, meaning "one who squirts." Algonquian is a language spoken by the Abenaki, who are a tribe of American Indian and First Nations people in northeastern North America.

The skunk family is divided into five groups: stink badgers and striped, hooded, spotted, and hog-nosed skunks. The Palawan stink badger lives only in the Philippines, and the Sunda stink badger lives only in Indonesia. All other skunks live in North America and Mexico. Striped skunks are common throughout the entire North American continent except in Alaska, but hooded skunks are limited to the southwestern United

In the language of the Abenaki, their name for themselves means "Real People" or simply "The People."

The four species of spotted skunks —more agile than striped or hog-nosed skunks— are the only skunks to hunt and forage in trees.

Least weasels—unlike their skunk relatives—actively hunt prey such as mice, voles, and young rabbits.

States. The four species of spotted skunk are found in the U.S. and Mexico, and the four species of hog-nosed skunk exist only in scattered locations in Colorado, New Mexico, Texas, and Mexico.

The smallest skunk relative is the least weasel, which weighs less than three ounces (85 g). The largest North American relative is the wolverine, which can weigh up to 50 pounds (22.7 kg). Skunks are much smaller than wolverines. As the largest skunks, striped and hooded skunks can be up to 29 inches (73.7 cm) in length and weigh about 8 pounds (3.6 kg). Hog-nosed skunks can be up to 26 inches (66 cm) long and 4 pounds (1.8 kg). Spotted skunks are the smallest North American skunks. They can grow to 21 inches (53.3 cm) in length and weigh only about 2 pounds (0.9 kg). The Sunda stink badger reaches no more than 20 inches (50.8 cm) in length but weighs up to 8 pounds (3.6 kg), and the slightly shorter Palawan stink badger averages about 5 pounds (2.3 kg).

A skunk has large feet with five toes on each foot and sharp claws that are useful for digging. It has a long tail—as long as the skunk's head and body combined. Skunks are nearsighted, meaning they can see things in

While wolverines primarily eat meat, they share skunks' taste for insect eggs, roots, seeds, and berries.

Homeowners are often dismayed with a skunk's ability to dig holes in lawns while searching for grubs.

close view, but they cannot see distant objects very clearly. Male skunks, called bucks, and female skunks, called does, are about the same size and the same color—black and white. Striped skunks are black with white stripes that run from nose to tail. Spotted skunks are black with white spots or broken stripes on the head, back, and tail. Hooded skunks have a white collar or band around the neck and white stripes on the back and tail. Hog-nosed skunks have a hairless snout. Their backs and tails are white, and the lower body and undersides are black.

Skunks are nocturnal animals, meaning they are most active at night. They may travel as far as three miles (4.8 km) each night in search of food. With good night vision, skunks are able to see in near darkness. The skunk's eyes are equipped with a reflective layer of tissue called a tapetum lucidum. This tissue collects light and concentrates it in the center of the **retina**, enabling a skunk to see much better than humans can in very low light. The tapetum lucidum causes eyeshine, a condition in which an animal's eyes reflect color when a light source is shined on them. The skunk's eyeshine is always bright white.

Skunks do not move quickly. In fact, their short legs and long body cause them to waddle. Skunks hunt by pouncing on prey and then using their sharp claws to keep the prey from escaping —similar to the way cats hunt. Skunks are seldom in a hurry to get anywhere, but when they do run, it looks more like leaping. Skunks push off with both back feet, stretch out their bodies, and reach forward with both front feet, landing with a bit of a bounce. Skunks cannot outrun most predators, yet they are generally fearless when threatened. They owe this confidence to their ability to spray attackers with unpleasant musk.

Skunks usually spray only as a last effort to avoid attack. They first face predators, hissing, stomping their front feet, and scratching the ground. If the predator does

A striped skunk's nearsightedness means it can clearly focus on an object no more than three feet (0.9 m) away.

Patterns of white markings on eastern spotted skunks vary among the animals and are used by researchers to identify individuals.

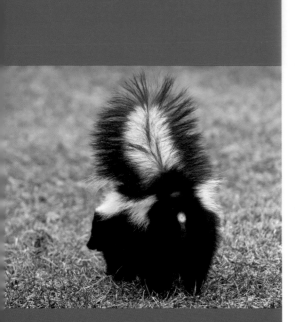

The underside of a skunk's tail is typically stained as a result of the yellowish musk the skunk sprays at enemies.

Studies have shown that high concentrations of skunk musk can be toxic, causing the victim to lose consciousness.

not retreat, the skunk then arches its back like a cat and raises its tail straight up. If an attacker is not deterred by these gestures, the skunk will turn its back and send a stream of musk toward its foe. To spray, two tiny nozzles thrust out of the skunk's anal opening. The nozzles operate independently of each other, so the skunk can control both the angle of the stream and the distance as well as whether the spray is a fine mist or a stream of heavy drops. Musk can be sprayed up to 10 feet (3 m).

The spotted skunk has an additional advantage when it comes to spraying musk: it does not need to turn its back on the predator. Instead, the spotted skunk can lean forward on its front feet and raise its back feet off the ground in a type of handstand. As it straightens its tail, dipping the tail down toward its nose, the skunk releases its musk in the direction that it is facing.

Skunks cannot carry an unlimited supply of musk. Special sacs on each side of the anus hold about two ounces (59 ml) of musk apiece. If the musk is used up during an encounter with a predator, the skunk will need time to produce more. While skunks are not aware when their scent sacs are empty, skunks rarely spray so much as to

empty them entirely. One squirt is usually all it takes to send a predator running. Skunk musk is an oily, yellowish liquid made up of three types of **sulfur** compounds that cause a burning sensation on the skin. Skunks are immune to the irritation caused by their musk, but potential predators, if squirted in the face, typically run away with painful, swollen eyes and blurred vision that lasts for 15 minutes or more after contact. In addition, the odor of skunk spray can be detected as far as 1.5 miles (2.4 km) from the source, deterring other predators as well.

Animals that share skunk habitat learn to avoid encounters with skunks once they have been sprayed.

Skunks investigate fallen, dead trees because the softening logs are havens for insect activity.

RAISING A STINK

Skunks may be some of the most widely distributed mammals in North America, but they are solitary creatures that do not live in communities with each other. They live in dens abandoned by other animals or inside hollow logs or dead standing trees near food and water sources. Natural skunk habitats range from open pastures and prairies to dense forests. Skunks have **adapted** to life in farming and urban areas as well, commonly establishing homes under stone walls, porches, or rock piles; inside barns, garages, and sheds; and even in dense shrubbery near houses and other buildings. Skunks do not like bright lights or noise, so they typically choose den sites that are isolated, abandoned, or at least relatively quiet and undisturbed.

Skunks are omnivorous, meaning they eat both animals and plants. They eat more plant matter in the fall and winter, when berries, fallen apples, and leftover grain from harvesting are abundant. In spring and summer, skunks prefer to feed on insects such as grasshoppers, crickets, and beetles. In winter, skunks hunt mice and rats, and when other food is scarce,

Skunks eat continuously throughout the summer to build a thick layer of fat that will sustain them over the winter.

A skunk's characteristic markings are present from birth and become more pronounced as the animal ages.

Skunks' distinctive coloration and markings are aposematic, which means that other animals are warned away from them.

skunks may even hunt rabbits. Skunks also eat eggs and often raid the nests of ground-dwelling birds and waterfowl. If a skunk is very hungry, it may eat rotting flesh. Despite the popular perception that skunks are **nuisance** animals, Montana State University in Bozeman reported that only 5 percent of a skunk's diet is made up of farm products that are valuable to humans. While skunks may occasionally eat corn from fields, raid beehives, and steal eggs from chicken coops, skunks actually benefit farmers more often than not by eating damaging insects, mice, and rats.

A skunk typically establishes a home range that varies from .5 to 2 miles (0.8–3.2 km) in diameter and contains up to 10 dens. Home ranges shrink in winter and expand in spring and summer. Also, larger skunk species tend to establish larger home ranges. Seeking food and water, a skunk patrols its home range regularly, and while skunks' home ranges may overlap each other, skunks generally stay out of each other's way, except during courtship and mating. Male skunks may travel as far as five miles (8 km) outside their home ranges each night in search of mates during mating season.

Both male and female skunks can reproduce when they are about 10 months old. The mating season in North America runs from late February through late March. Males are attracted to females by their scent. In preparation for mating, males and females chase each other. Then the male bites the female on the back of the neck to begin mating. They will mate many times to ensure success. Skunks typically give birth once a year, but on rare occasions, skunks will have a second litter (group of young) in the same year.

Wild turkey eggs have high nutritional value to a skunk, which seeks out and raids unprotected nests.

Young skunks often combine foraging with play, which helps them develop necessary survival skills.

During times of extended winter, when spring vegetation is delayed, a female skunk that becomes pregnant may put the **embryos** "on hold" for a period of several weeks. During this time, called embryonic diapause, the baby skunks, called kits, stop developing until environmental conditions improve. This suspension ensures that the kits will have a food source when they are ready to eat plants and insects.

Before she gives birth, the female skunk selects a protected place, such as a deep log or dense bush, where she and her offspring will be safest from predators. The female lines the den with soft plants and leaves. After 60 to 75 days, the female gives birth to a litter of kits. Typical litters have 4 to 6 kits, but first-time mothers may give birth to as few as 2, while experienced mothers may have up to 16 kits in a litter. Weighing only about one ounce (28.3 g) at birth, kits are born ready to spray, though their musk is weak. They are born blind with hairless skin that bears the striped or spotted markings of the fur they will later develop. They immediately begin feeding on the milk produced by their mother. At about four weeks of age, the kits open their eyes and develop the ability to spray musk. At this age, the kits become playfully curious with each other. Striped skunks stay close to the ground, but spotted skunks tend to climb over logs, rocks, and even fences. Curious spotted skunks have even been known to climb buildings and make dens in attics.

At about seven weeks old, the kits begin to follow their mother around as she forages, learning by her example how to select food and hunt prey. By two months old, the kits are fully **weaned**. They remain in their mother's den until late July or early August. Then, at about five months

Skunk enthusiasts consider baby skunks to be among the most curious and playful of all small mammal species.

Unlike solitary wild skunks, domesticated skunks are content to live in small groups where food is easy to come by.

Mother skunks rarely leave their kits alone in the den because male skunks—even the kits' own fathers—may kill babies.

old, they leave their family to establish a home range, build a den, and forage food for themselves. After five or six more months, the skunks will be fully mature and ready to start the cycle of mating and producing offspring.

In the winter, in areas where the weather is cold, skunks may spend the coldest month in a state of torpor, which is a kind of temporary hibernation in which the body system slows down and the animal sleeps. These periods of winter rest often drive skunks together to share dens for warmth. A group of skunks is called a surfeit (*SER-fit*)—a word that means "an excessive amount." For many of the skunk's neighboring animals, one skunk— much less an entire group of skunks—is too many. Yet despite their defensive ability, many young, old, and sick skunks fall prey to coyotes, wolves, mountain lions, and owls. A healthy skunk's greatest threat is humans. Because they are slow-moving and have poor eyesight, skunks often fall victim to traffic collisions. In fact, skunks have been wiped out of many areas where automobile traffic is particularly heavy. Skunks in captivity can live about 10 years, but in the wild, skunks typically do not live more than 3 or 4 years.

A skunk mother will gently bite the nape, or back, of her offspring's neck to move or carry it.

Chemically processed animal skins with the fur still attached are called pelts, and skunk pelts are not worth much money.

PARFUM DE SKUNK

Many American Indian **cultures** have traditionally admired the skunk for its fearless self-defense. The oral tradition of the Muskogee Creek includes stories about skunks defending their families from various threats and punishing other animals that had misbehaved. The Cherokee believed that skunks possessed magical powers and that the odor could ward off disease; often a dead skunk was hung over the doorway of a sick person's home. Other tribes viewed skunks as dangerous, untrustworthy creatures. In the Ojibwa tradition, Aniwye is the Skunk Spirit—a giant skunk with poisonous musk and a violent temper. One story tells how a village of people learned that Aniwye was coming to destroy their homes, so the people quickly packed up and left. A sick, old woman stayed behind, and when Aniwye tore the roof off her house and demanded she tell where everyone else had gone, she refused. Aniwye sprayed her with musk, killing her. While the skunk is portrayed unrealistically as an aggressor to humans, the story shows how the selfless sacrifice of one person saved an entire village of people.

Stink badgers are called *stinkdachs* by Germans, *stinkgraevling* by Norwegians, and *tasso odoroso* by Italians.

Processed skunk musk is used in some perfumes to help the scent last longer than it would if the perfume contained only water or alcohol.

In popular culture, skunks are often portrayed as silly, inquisitive creatures with friendly personalities. Readers of *Ranger Rick*, a monthly nature magazine published by the National Wildlife Foundation, can follow the adventures of Odora (nicknamed Odie) the skunk. In one story, Odie joins Ranger Rick and Boomer Badger for a day at the beach to visit their friend Sheldon Sea Turtle. Upon finding the beach littered with trash, Odie picks up a plastic bag and gets everyone to help clean up the beach. Odie also rescues a seabird that is tangled in the string of a discarded balloon, and the gang goes surfing.

Jimmy Skunk, a character created by American author and conservationist Thornton Burgess, first appeared in the book *Old Mother West Wind* in 1910. Burgess wrote more than 15,000 stories in his lifetime—mostly about animals such as Jimmy Skunk—to teach lessons about the values of compassion, forgiveness, and sharing. Burgess's books are still in print today, and the Kidoons Network hosts a number of websites based on characters in Burgess's books, including Jimmy Skunk. Visitors to www.jimmyskunk.com will find coloring pages, e-cards, image downloads, games, and stories about Jimmy Skunk.

One of the world's best-loved skunk characters is Flower, from the classic 1942 Walt Disney movie *Bambi*. In the film, a young deer, Bambi, grows up in the forest with many friends, including Thumper the rabbit, who teaches Bambi the names of things. While exploring a patch of flowers, Bambi meets a young striped skunk, whom he calls Flower. The skunk gratefully accepts the

Flower is a shy character that teaches Bambi a lesson about friendship and trust in the movie Bambi.

When Boog the grizzly bear unknowingly insults skunks Rosie and Maria in Open Season, he gets sprayed.

name, and so begins a lifelong friendship between Bambi and Flower. Later, Flower meets a female striped skunk. The two become mates, and at the end of the film, they show off to Bambi their family of kits.

Other animated skunks include Stella from *Over the Hedge* (2006), Rosie and Maria from *Open Season* (2006), and Reeko from *Stuart Little 3: Call of the Wild* (2006). Canadian television features a number of skunks, including Spiff the skunk from the show *Iggy Arbuckle*, which aired for one season in 2007 but can still be found occasionally on the Cartoon Network. Also, Skunk, from the long-running

TV show *Franklin*, which was based on the Franklin the Turtle books by Brenda Clark and Paulette Bourgeois, made his debut in 1997. When the Nickelodeon Canada channel launched in 2009, it picked up the show *Angry Beavers* (1997–2003), which featured a recurring skunk character.

A skunk named Stinky, who appeared in the 1945 Warner Bros. cartoon *Odor-able Kitty*, was the earliest incarnation of one of the best-known striped skunks in the world: French-speaking Pepé Le Pew of the *Looney Tunes* and *Merrie Melodies* cartoons. A romantic at heart, Pepé constantly chases female skunks—as well as black-and-white cats that look like skunks. In the cartoon *Really Scent*, a female cat named Penelope has a birthmark that leaves her with a white stripe. All the male cats reject her because she looks like a skunk, which makes her the perfect match for Pepé, who pursues her relentlessly.

The tables are turned for Pepé in *For Scent-Imental Reasons*, when Pepé's stripe is accidentally painted black. Penelope, made unattractive to Pepé because she has been dunked in dirty water and sneezes with a head cold, chases Pepé through a perfume factory. Pepé has also appeared in *Tiny Toon Adventures*, *Tweety's High-Flying Adventure*, and

Pepé has appeared as a balloon at Canada's annual Atlantic International Balloon Fiesta in Sussex, New Brunswick.

Polecats have been known to paralyze prey with a bite to the brain and store the meat for later consumption.

Veterinarians at Cornell University developed an oral rabies vaccine in 2006 that can be given to skunks in food pellets.

the 1996 film *Space Jam*. Pepé has most recently appeared as a regular cast member of *The Looney Tunes Show*, which premiered on the Cartoon Network in 2011. Also from Warner Bros., Fifi La Fume is a purple striped skunk featured in *Tiny Toon Adventures*. With a pink ribbon in her hair and romance in her heart, the teenaged cheerleader has chased Furball the cat, Calamity Coyote, and Hamton J. Pig with a passion similar to Pepé Le Pew's.

A cartoon skunk is the mascot for a serious branch of industry in the U.S.: Lockheed Martin's Advanced Development Programs, which is nicknamed "Skunk Works." In business and industry, the term "skunkworks" is used to describe a department or laboratory that is free to work outside normal company restrictions or on secret projects. One of Lockheed Martin's Skunk Works projects was the Polecat, an unmanned aircraft designed to carry weapons or surveillance equipment, which debuted in 2005. The aircraft was named after wild skunks, which are sometimes called polecats. (True polecats consist of four species in the weasel family).

Sports teams are typically named for ferocious or powerful animals, and skunks generally do not fit the bill.

The closest skunks have come to being mascots is through association with polecats. The State University of New York (SUNY) Potsdam Polecats are the school's men's and women's rugby clubs, and in Australia, the Norwest Polecats rugby league club was established in 1971. The Monticello Polecats are an amateur baseball team from Minnesota, and the Albany Polecats were a minor-league baseball team in Georgia through 1995 (after which they moved to Maryland and became the Shorebirds). In general, the word "skunk" is often negatively associated with being small and smelly—not the sort of image that most groups want to promote.

LASRE, an engine pod attached to the back of a Blackbird aircraft, was a research-gathering tool used by NASA's Skunk Works in the 1990s.

JIMMY SKUNK IS VERY MAD INDEED

Now when Jimmy Skunk is angry, he doesn't bite and he doesn't scratch. You know Old Mother Nature has provided him with a little bag of perfume which Jimmy doesn't object to in the least, but which makes most people want to hold their noses and run. He never uses it, excepting when he is angry or in danger, but when he does use it, his enemies always turn tail and run. That is why he is afraid of no one, and why every one respects Jimmy and his rights.

He used it now, and he didn't waste any time about it. He threw some of that perfume right in the face of Reddy Fox before Reddy had a chance to turn or to say a word.

"Take that!" snapped Jimmy Skunk. "Perhaps it will teach you not to play tricks on your honest neighbors!"

Poor Reddy! Some of that perfume got in his eyes and made them smart dreadfully. In fact, for a little while he couldn't see at all. And then the smell of it was so strong that it made him quite sick. He rolled over and over on the ground, choking and gasping and rubbing his eyes. Jimmy Skunk just stood and looked on, and there wasn't a bit of pity in his eyes.

"How do you like that?" said he. "You thought yourself very smart, rolling me down hill in a barrel, didn't you? You might have broken my neck."

excerpt from The Adventures of Jimmy Skunk, *by Thornton Burgess (1874-1965)*

SWEET SMELL OF SUCCESS

A thick winter pelage, or coat of fur, protects skunks from the cold and wind as they prepare for hibernation.

Skunks are resilient animals, surviving in a wide variety of habitats, eating just about anything that is small enough to be devoured, and reproducing in healthy numbers. However, like many small mammals, skunks can carry one of the most feared diseases in the animal world: rabies, a disease affecting the brain that is fatal in animals and can be fatal in humans if left untreated. Of all North American mammals, skunks have the second-highest rate of rabies infection after raccoons. A skunk that is behaving aggressively, walking in circles, making wobbling or dancing movements, and biting at itself could be rabid. Rabies is transmitted through saliva, typically by biting. While a healthy skunk rarely bites other animals that it does not intend to eat—including humans—a rabid skunk can viciously attack for apparently no reason.

To avoid spreading the disease to other animals or people, animal control professionals must put down rabid skunks. While **domestic** animals can be vaccinated against rabies infection, humans who are bitten by rabid animals must undergo treatment by injections to prevent illness.

Because of predation and difficulty finding food in winter, nearly 90 percent of skunks die within their first year of life.

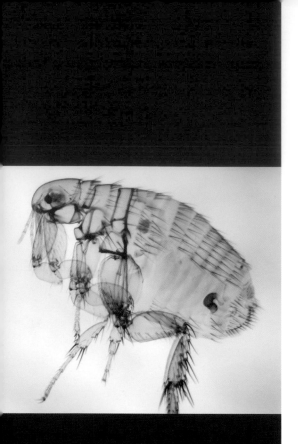

In addition to being vaccinated for rabies and distemper, pet skunks should be treated regularly for fleas (pictured above) and parasites.

In the U.S., the last reported case of a person contracting rabies from a skunk was in 1981. Wildlife biologists such as Samantha M. Wisely, a professor at Kansas State University, observe striped skunks in the wild to research rabies. They also study the **genetic** material of infected animals. Wisely's research centers around genetic changes that occur in the rabies virus when it is transmitted from one animal to another—research that may one day lead to a reduction in the spread of the deadly disease.

Distemper is another serious disease that afflicts dogs, cats, and other small mammals, including skunks. Attacking an animal's nervous system, distemper causes difficulty breathing, muscle spasms, and even **paralysis**. The distemper virus grows in an animal's respiratory mucus and is transmitted when an infected animal licks, coughs, or sneezes on other animals. There is no cure for distemper, but, like rabies, the disease can be prevented with regular vaccinations.

Skunks suffering from rabies or distemper typically cease grooming, which leads to serious flea, mite, and tick infestations. Fleas can drain a skunk of blood; mites can cause a painful disease called scabies (also known as mange), which

A flea infestation can cause a skunk to lose its fur and develop sores on its skin.

makes the skin bleed and the hair fall out; and ticks can carry a number of blood diseases, including Lyme disease. Skunks are often affected by **parasites** such as roundworms and tapeworms, which steal **nutrients** from an infected skunk's digestive system, leading to the animal's death.

Despite the skunk's susceptibility to disease, skunks are beneficial animals to farmers and gardeners because they eat many agricultural pests, from potato beetles and cutworms to mice, rats, and moles. While many landowners choose to leave skunks on their property undisturbed, they then run the risk of being surprised by them. Dogs are especially vulnerable to skunks because dogs may startle skunks or corner them—actions that may compel skunks to spray. Skunk musk may cling to dog fur for weeks or months. Experts agree that if a dog is sprayed, the best recipe for making a solution that will neutralize the odor is to mix one quart of 3 percent hydrogen peroxide with one-quarter cup of baking soda and one teaspoon of detergent. This concoction should be mixed outdoors—never indoors. The dog should be bathed in the mixture, avoiding the dog's eyes, for at least five minutes before being rinsed.

One man has been skunk-sprayed so many times he has lost count. Jerry Dragoo, a biology professor at the University of New Mexico in Albuquerque, began studying skunks as a college student. The first time he was sprayed, he could not understand what all the fuss was about—he did not smell anything out of the ordinary. But when he returned to his college lab three days later, his colleagues tossed him out of the building. It turned out that Dragoo was one of the less than 6 percent of people in the world who lack a sense of smell. Today, he operates the Dragoo Institute for the Betterment of Skunks and Skunk Reputations in Tijeras, New Mexico. He and his wife,

Skunks may raid vegetable gardens not only for vegetables but also for the grubs and insects there.

Skunks use their front claws to hold down venomous snakes' heads while delivering a killing bite to the back of the neck.

Hog-nosed skunks overturn rocks with their noses to access the food sources hidden beneath.

Gwen, a veterinary technician, take in orphaned, injured, and abandoned skunks, rehabilitating and releasing those they can. Dragoo's extensive research on skunks led to the discovery that skunks are not directly related to weasels.

Because skunks can be de-scented by having their anal glands surgically removed, de-scented skunks are popular as pets in North America and Europe. Not all pet skunks are de-scented, though. Only 17 U.S. states allow people to own skunks as pets, and laws vary in other parts of the world. For example, the surgical de-scenting of skunks has recently become illegal in the United Kingdom. **Captive-breeding** of skunks has occurred for more than 60 years, with skunk fanciers selectively breeding skunks to achieve a variety of designer colors, from champagne, lavender, and apricot to silver, smoke, and blue-gray. Skunks are challenging pets because they are insatiably curious. They dig and explore everywhere, with no regard for furniture or barriers such as closed doors. Experts caution that only the most experienced—and tolerant—of pet owners should attempt keeping a skunk.

Deborah Cipriani founded Skunk Haven in North Ridgeville, Ohio, in 2004 as a sanctuary for skunks that have

A skunk is born with front claws that are well equipped for digging; these grow more powerful over time.

Skunks constantly survey their surroundings for food and are especially eager to raid beehives for honey.

been abandoned by frustrated owners. Skunk Haven also provides education and support for people who own skunks or are considering keeping or breeding skunks. Skunk Haven rescues about 60 skunks each year from around the U.S. and abroad. Skunk Haven also sponsors Skunk Fest, an annual gathering of skunk fanciers who share information and show off their skunks. Similar rehabilitation and education groups are located across the U.S. and include the Society of Kind Understanding and Not Killing Skunks (SKUNKS), located in Lancaster, California, and the Walkin' Wild Skunk Rescue in Paradise, Texas.

Since skunks are capable of successfully adapting to changing environments, most skunk species enjoy healthy populations. Only the pygmy spotted skunk is currently categorized on the International Union for Conservation of Nature (IUCN) Red List of Threatened Species as vulnerable, which means there are factors that could lead to this species' **extinction** in the wild. With further research and education that exposes the true nature of skunks as timid, beneficial animals undeserving of their stinky reputations, perhaps humans can help these amazing mammals continue to thrive.

Regardless of a skunk's "designer" color, it will retain its stripes, which can be faint or bright white.

ANIMAL TALE: THE FIRST SKUNK

Like all cultures of the world, American Indian cultures are rich in myths and folk tales. The Ho-Chunk Indians of Wisconsin and northern Illinois have a strong bond with their native land and its wildlife, which their mythology reflects. This story tells how the first skunk came to be.

Long ago, a kind and beautiful woman lived in the village, and she gave birth to the most beautiful infant anyone had ever seen. As the girl grew older, she also became more beautiful. Her skin glowed like fine copper, her eyes glistened like agates, and her hair shimmered white as snow.

But the more beautiful she grew, the more vain she became. She spent hours brushing her white hair and gazing at her image in pools of still water, marveling at herself. She loved to smell good, too, so she picked the finest flowers and herbs to rub all over her skin and hair. As a young woman, she decided that no one in the world was as lovely as she was.

When the time came for the young woman to choose a husband, many young men tried to impress her. While she did not want to consider marriage (for she was too vain to believe that anyone was worthy enough), the young woman agreed to meet the suitors who lined up to court her. One man brought her a crown of fragrant flowers to wear in her hair, but she immediately dismissed him. Another brought her colorful beads to wear around her neck, and likewise she sent him away. A third man brought her cedar oil to scent her hair, but she threw his gift back at him.

"How dare you insult me by suggesting that I need anything to make myself more beautiful," she told them all.

One day, a grizzled old man came to the young woman. He had no gift for her, yet he asked her to consider only the purity of his love and his promise to care for her always. She laughed at the old man. "You are ugly," she said to him. "I am the most beautiful woman in the world. I could never take you as my husband."

What the young woman did not know was that the old man was not who he appeared to be. Under his disguise, Turtle, one of the great spirits, was hidden. "Try to see beneath my appearance," Turtle said to the young woman. "It is important that you see beauty on the inside and not only the outside."

"Go away!" the young woman shouted. "You do not deserve me."

With that, Turtle shed his disguise and stood before the young woman. His beauty made her look away, ashamed. "It is *you* who does not deserve *me*," Turtle replied. "Since you failed to try to understand the lesson I imparted, you will be transformed." The young woman instantly began to shrink, and black hair sprouted upon her body. "When people see you," Turtle went on, "they will run away from your repulsive odor."

Small, and left with only a narrow streak of white hair on a body covered with black fur, the young woman became the first skunk—a shy creature with no vanity.

GLOSSARY

adapted – changed to improve its chances of survival in its environment

captive-breeding – being bred and raised in a place from which escape is not possible

cultures – particular groups in a society that share behaviors and characteristics that are accepted as normal by that group

domestic – tamed to be kept as a pet or used as a work animal

embryos – unborn or unhatched offspring in the early stages of development

extinction – the act or process of becoming extinct; coming to an end or dying out

genetic – relating to genes, the basic physical units of heredity

mammals – warm-blooded animals that have a backbone and hair or fur, give birth to live young, and produce milk to feed their young

musk – a strong-smelling liquid substance produced by some mammals such as weasels, seals, and skunks

myths – beliefs or stories that explain how something came to be or that are associated with a person or object

nuisance – something annoying or harmful to people or the land

nutrients – substances that can be used by an animal to give energy and build tissue

paralysis – loss of muscle movement

parasites – animals or plants that live on or inside another living thing (called a host) while giving nothing back to the host; some parasitic organisms cause disease or even death

retina – a layer or lining in the back of the eye that is sensitive to light

sulfur – a yellow-colored element found in various rocks and gases

weaned – made the young of a mammal accept food other than nursing milk

SELECTED BIBLIOGRAPHY

Bowers, Nora, Rick Bowers, and Kenn Kaufman. *Kaufman Field Guide to Mammals of North America*. 12th ed. New York: Houghton Mifflin, 2007.

Cole, Nigel. *Is That Skunk?* DVD. Washington, D.C.: Corporation for Public Broadcasting, 2009.

Gehrt, Stanley D., Seth P. D. Riley, and Brian L. Cypher, eds. *Urban Carnivores: Ecology, Conflict, and Conservation*. Baltimore: Johns Hopkins University Press, 2010.

Kays, Roland W., and Don E. Wilson. *Mammals of North America*. 2nd ed. Princeton, N.J.: Princeton University Press, 2009.

Merritt, Joseph F. *The Biology of Small Mammals*. Baltimore: Johns Hopkins University Press, 2010.

Wilke, Christopher J. "*Mephitis mephitis*." Animal Diversity Web. http://animaldiversity.ummz.umich.edu/accounts/Mephitis_mephitis/.

Skunks may borrow the vacant burrows of coyotes, foxes, or raccoons during the summer when they are foraging.

INDEX

Burgess, Thornton 28, 34

cultural influences 27, 28, 29–31, 32, 44
    aircraft 32
    fictional characters 28
    films and cartoons 29–30, 31, 32
    folk tales 27, 44
    symbolic importance 27
    television 30–31, 32

diet 7–8, 11, 15, 19–20, 22, 23, 24, 35, 38
    plants and fruits 7–8, 19, 22, 23
    prey 15, 19–20, 22, 23, 38
    water 20

habitats 7, 11, 12, 19, 20, 21, 24, 35, 38
    Asia 11
    forests 19
    and home ranges 20, 24
    Mexico 11, 12
    near humans 19, 38
    North America 11, 12, 19, 21
    prairies 19

hog-nosed skunks 10, 11, 12, 14

hooded skunks 10, 11, 12, 14

kits 22, 23, 24, 30
    appearance at birth 23
    litter size 23

life spans 24, 35

mating 20, 21–22, 24, 30
    and embryonic diapause 22

Mephitinae family 11

movement and speed 15, 24, 35

pet skunks 36, 40, 43
    and Skunk Haven 40, 43

physical characteristics 11, 12, 14, 15, 16, 17, 20, 23, 24, 39
    claws 12, 15, 39
    colors and markings 14, 15, 20, 23
    eyes and vision 12, 14, 15, 24
    musk 11, 15, 16, 17, 23, 39
    sizes 12, 14, 23
    tails 12, 14, 16

populations 43

predators 8, 15, 16, 17, 23, 24
    coyotes 24
    mountain lions 24
    owls 8, 24
    wolves 24

relatives 11, 12, 32, 40
    weasels 11, 12, 32, 40
    wolverines 12

scientific studies 20, 36, 39–40, 43
    by Jerry Dragoo 39–40
    by Samantha M. Wisely 36

solitary behavior 19, 20

spotted skunks 10, 11, 12, 14, 15, 16, 23, 43

stink badgers 10, 11, 12, 27

striped skunks 10, 11, 12, 14, 23, 29, 30, 36

threats 24, 35–36, 38
    automobiles 24
    blood diseases 38
    distemper 36
    parasites 38
    rabies 35–36
    scabies 36

torpor 24